Our favorite
Comfort Food recipes

Copyright 2010, Gooseberry Patch

Previously published under ISBN 978-1-93628-308-8

Cover: Easy Chicken Pot Pie (page 21)

Lots of favorite comfort foods are made with buttermilk.
If there's none on hand, just stir 3/4 cup plain yogurt
with 1/4 cup milk and let stand for a few minutes...simple!

Buttermilk Cinnamon Rolls

Makes one dozen

3 c. all-purpose flour
4 t. baking powder
1/4 t. baking soda
1 t. salt
1/2 c. shortening

1-1/2 c. buttermilk
1/2 c. butter, softened
1/2 c. sugar
1/2 t. cinnamon

Combine first 4 ingredients; cut in shortening until crumbs form. Stir in buttermilk until well blended; knead dough on a lightly floured surface for 4 to 5 minutes. Roll out to 1/4-inch thickness; spread butter over dough to edges. In a small bowl, mix sugar and cinnamon; sprinkle over dough. Roll up jelly-roll style; cut into 1/2-inch slices. Place on a greased baking sheet; bake at 450 degrees for 10 to 12 minutes.

Keep all your hot chocolate must-haves together in
a vintage serving tray. Mini marshmallows, whipped cream,
shakers of cinnamon or cocoa and peppermint sticks
will be right at your fingertips.

Hot Chocolate Supreme

1 c. sugar
1/2 c. baking cocoa
1/4 t. salt
5 c. water
2 c. milk

1 c. whipping cream
Garnish: marshmallows,
    whipped topping, crushed
    peppermint candies

Combine sugar, cocoa and salt in a medium saucepan; whisk in water.
Bring to a boil over high heat, stirring until sugar is completely
dissolved. Reduce heat to medium; add milk and cream. Heat
through; keep warm over low heat. Serve topped with marshmallows
or whipped topping and sprinkled with crushed peppermint candies.

Tuck odds & ends of leftover sliced bread, croissants
and even cinnamon rolls into a freezer container. Before long,
you'll have enough for delicious French toast!

Golden French Toast

Serves 8 to 10

1 loaf white bread, cubed
   and divided
8-oz. pkg. cream cheese,
   softened and cubed

10 eggs, beaten
1-1/2 c. half-and-half
1/2 c. butter, melted
1/4 c. maple syrup

Layer half the bread in a greased 13"x9" baking pan; top with cream
cheese. Place remaining bread over the top; set aside. Beat eggs,
half-and-half, butter and syrup together; pour over bread. Refrigerate
overnight; bake at 350 degrees for 40 to 50 minutes.

Enjoy a leisurely breakfast with your family...at dinnertime!
Cheesy Bacon Casserole is perfect. Just add a basket of
muffins, fresh fruit and a steamy pot of tea.

Cheesy Bacon Casserole

Makes 4 servings

4 slices white bread, crusts
    trimmed
4 eggs, beaten
1-1/2 c. milk
1 t. dry mustard

1/2 t. dried, chopped onion
8 slices bacon, crisply cooked
    and crumbled
1 c. shredded Cheddar cheese

Arrange bread slices in a lightly greased 8"x8" baking pan; set aside.
Stir together eggs, milk, mustard and onion; pour over bread. Sprinkle
with bacon; cover and refrigerate 8 hours or overnight. Let stand at
room temperature for 30 minutes; uncover and bake at 350 degrees
for 20 to 25 minutes. Sprinkle with cheese and bake an additional
5 minutes, until cheese melts.

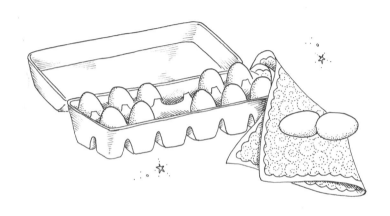

Buttery cinnamon toast warms you right up on a chilly morning. Spread softened butter generously on one side of toasted bread and sprinkle with cinnamon-sugar. Broil for one to 2 minutes, until hot and bubbly.

Miss Karen's Coffee Cake

Makes 12 servings

2 c. all-purpose flour
2 c. brown sugar, packed
3/4 c. butter, diced
8-oz. container sour cream
1 egg, beaten
1 t. vanilla extract

1/4 t. ground ginger
1 t. baking soda
3 T. sugar
1 t. cinnamon
1 c. chopped pecans

Mix together flour and brown sugar in a large bowl; cut in butter until crumbly. Press 2-3/4 cups of mixture into a greased 13"x9" baking pan; set aside remaining mixture. In a separate bowl, combine sour cream, egg, vanilla, ginger and baking soda; add remaining crumbly mixture. Pour over crust. In a small bowl, combine sugar, cinnamon and pecans; sprinkle over sour cream mixture. Bake at 350 degrees for 25 to 30 minutes.

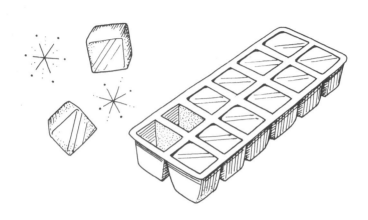

Freeze extra homemade chicken broth in ice cube trays for terrific flavor when making rice. Broth ice cubes are also handy when whipping up gravies or sauces.

Creamed Chicken

Makes 4 servings

4 boneless, skinless chicken
   breasts
1/2 c. butter
10 T. all-purpose flour

3-1/2 c. milk
4 to 6 cubes chicken bouillon
pepper to taste
4 biscuits, split

In a stockpot over medium heat, place chicken and enough water to cover. Simmer until juices run clear when chicken is pierced, about 20 minutes. Remove chicken from stockpot, reserving 3-1/2 cups broth. Set chicken aside until cool; cut into bite-size pieces. In a saucepan, melt butter and slowly add flour, stirring constantly until thickened. Gradually add reserved broth; continue stirring until thickened. Pour milk into mixture; add bouillon, chicken and pepper. Cook until bouillon is dissolved. Serve over split biscuits.

For a healthy change, give whole-wheat noodles a try
in your favorite casserole...they taste great and
contain more fiber than regular noodles.

Tuna Noodle Casserole

Serves 6

16-oz. pkg. wide egg noodles,
  cooked
2 10-3/4 oz. cans cream of
  mushroom soup
1 to 2 6-oz. cans tuna, drained
1 c. frozen peas, thawed

4-oz. can sliced mushrooms,
  drained
1 to 2 c. milk
salt and pepper to taste
8-oz. pkg. shredded Cheddar
  cheese

Combine noodles, soup, tuna, peas and mushrooms; stir in enough milk to moisten well. Add salt and pepper to taste. Spread in a lightly greased 13"x9" baking pan; sprinkle with cheese. Bake, uncovered, at 350 degrees for 25 minutes, until hot and bubbly.

Fix a double batch! Cook meatballs according to the recipe,
freeze individually on baking sheets, then store in
a freezer-safe container until ready to use.

Meatballs & Sauce

Serves 4

1 lb. ground beef
1 c. soft bread crumbs
2 eggs, beaten
1/2 c. grated Parmesan cheese
3 T. fresh Italian parsley,
    chopped
1. T. garlic powder

1 t. salt
1 t. pepper
2 to 4 T. olive oil
2 28-oz. cans crushed tomatoes
dried basil to taste
cooked spaghetti or hard rolls

In a large bowl, mix ground beef, bread crumbs, eggs, Parmesan cheese and seasonings. Form into 2-inch balls. In a large skillet over medium-high heat, fry meatballs in oil, browning on all sides. Place meatballs in a large pot; add tomatoes. Simmer over low heat for at least an hour, stirring frequently. Add basil as desired. Serve meatballs and sauce over cooked spaghetti, or spoon into hard rolls to serve as sandwiches.

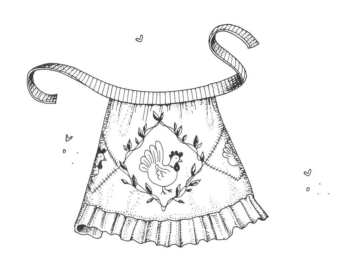

Often, for the tastiest country cooking, no fancy tools are needed...dig right in and mix that meatloaf with your hands!

Just Like Mom's Meatloaf

Serves 6

2 eggs, beaten
8-oz. can tomato sauce
3/4 c. cracker crumbs
1/4 c. onion, chopped
1/4 c. green pepper, finely
    chopped
1 T. Worcestershire sauce

1 t. salt
1/2 t. pepper
1-1/2 lbs. ground beef
1/2 c. catsup
2 t. mustard
2 T. brown sugar, packed

Combine first 8 ingredients in a bowl; add ground beef and mix well. Shape into a loaf; place in an ungreased 9"x5" loaf pan. Bake, uncovered, at 350 degrees for one hour. Combine catsup, mustard and brown sugar; spoon over meatloaf and bake an additional 10 to 15 minutes.

Make mini pot pies! Spoon filling into oven-safe bowls and
cut crust circles to fit, using another bowl as a guide.
Set on a baking sheet. Bake for 20 to 25 minutes at
400 degrees, until bubbly and golden.

Easy Chicken Pot Pie

2 8-oz. cans chicken, drained
2 13-1/4 oz. cans mixed
   vegetables, drained
2 10-3/4 oz. cans cream of
   chicken soup

1 c. milk
salt and pepper to taste
8-oz. pkg. shredded Cheddar
   or Colby cheese, divided
12-oz. tube refrigerated biscuits

In a bowl, combine all ingredients except cheese and biscuits. Transfer to a greased 13"x9" baking pan; top with 3/4 of cheese. Separate biscuits and tear each into 4 to 5 pieces; place on top of cheese. Sprinkle with remaining cheese. Bake, uncovered, at 350 degrees for 45 minutes, or until biscuits are golden.

Pairing a main dish with a salad? Give the salad
a fresh new taste...instead of using white vinegar to make
salad dressing, add a splash of fruit-flavored vinegar.

Deep-Dish Sausage Pizza

Makes 8 servings

16-oz. pkg. frozen bread
    dough, thawed
1 lb. sweet Italian pork sausage,
    casings removed
2 c. shredded mozzarella cheese
1 green pepper, cut into squares
1 red pepper, cut into squares

28-oz. can diced tomatoes,
    drained
3/4 t. dried oregano
1/2 t. salt
1/4 t. garlic powder
1/2 c. grated Parmesan cheese

Press thawed dough into the bottom and up the sides of a greased
13"x9" baking pan; set aside. In a large skillet, crumble sausage and
cook until no longer pink; drain. Sprinkle sausage over dough; top
with mozzarella cheese. In the same skillet, sauté peppers until
slightly tender. Stir in tomatoes with juice and seasonings; spoon
over pizza. Sprinkle with Parmesan cheese. Bake, uncovered, at
350 degrees for 25 to 35 minutes, until crust is golden.

A quick & easy seasoning mix is six parts salt to one part pepper.
Keep it close to the stove in a large shaker...so handy when
pan-frying pork chops or chicken!

Golden Breaded Pork Chops

Serves 8 to 10

1/2 c. dry bread crumbs
1/4 c. grated Parmesan cheese
1 T. dried oregano
1 t. dried marjoram
2 eggs, beaten

3-1/2 lb. boneless center-cut
   pork roast, sliced into
   1-1/2 inch chops
1/2 c. olive oil
salt and pepper to taste

Mix bread crumbs, Parmesan cheese and herbs in a shallow bowl;
set aside. Place eggs in a separate bowl. Dip pork chops into egg, then
into crumb mixture, reserving any remaining crumb mixture. Heat
oil in a deep skillet over medium-low heat. Cook chops for 5 to
7 minutes on each side until golden, adding salt and pepper to taste.

Ah! There is nothing like staying at home for real comfort.

-Jane Austen

Johnny Marzetti

Serves 4

1 lb. ground beef
1 onion, chopped
4-oz. can sliced mushrooms,
    drained
1/8 t. garlic salt
pepper to taste
1-1/2 T. sugar

2 15-oz. cans tomato sauce
1 T. Worcestershire sauce
8-oz. pkg. wide egg noodles,
    cooked and divided
8-oz. pkg. shredded sharp
    Cheddar cheese, divided

Cook ground beef, onion and mushrooms in a large skillet over medium heat; drain. Stir in garlic salt, pepper, sugar and sauces; simmer over low heat for 30 minutes. Layer half the noodles in a greased 2-quart casserole dish. Follow with a layer each of sauce and shredded cheese. Repeat layers. Bake, uncovered, at 375 degrees for 20 to 30 minutes, until hot and bubbly.

Ask family & friends to share a copy of tried & true recipe
favorites and create a special cookbook...a great gift
for a new cook in the family.

Better-than-Ever Beef Stroganoff

Serves 4

1-1/2 lbs. beef round steak,
    sliced into thin strips
1/4 c. all-purpose flour
pepper to taste
1/2 c. butter
4-oz. can sliced mushrooms,
    drained
1/2 c. onion, chopped

1 clove garlic, minced
10-1/2 oz. can beef broth
10-3/4 oz. can cream of
    mushroom soup
1 c. sour cream
8-oz. pkg. wide egg noodles,
    cooked

Coat beef strips with flour; sprinkle with pepper. Brown in a skillet
with butter; add mushrooms, onion and garlic. Sauté until tender; stir
in broth. Reduce heat; cover and simmer for one hour. Blend in soup
and sour cream; cook on low for about 5 minutes. Do not boil. Spoon
over cooked noodles to serve.

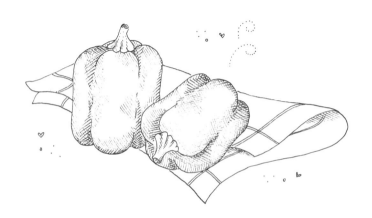

Perfectly cooked rice...as easy as 1-2-3! One cup long-cooking rice plus 2 cups water equals 3 cups cooked rice. Stir rice into boiling water, cover and simmer over low heat for 20 minutes. Leave the pan lid on for a few minutes more, then fluff with a fork.

Super-Easy Stuffed Peppers

Serves 4

4 green peppers, tops removed
1 lb. ground beef
1 onion, diced
3 T. Italian seasoning
1 clove garlic, pressed
3 c. cooked rice

26-oz. can spaghetti sauce,
   divided
salt and pepper to taste
Garnish: grated Parmesan
   cheese

Bring a large saucepan of water to a boil; add peppers and boil until
tender. Drain and set aside. Brown ground beef with onion in a skillet;
drain. Add Italian seasoning and garlic. Set aside 1/2 cup spaghetti
sauce. Combine ground beef mixture, remaining sauce, cooked rice,
salt and pepper in a bowl. Arrange peppers in a lightly greased
8"x8" baking pan. Fill peppers completely with ground beef mixture,
spooning any extra mixture between peppers. Top with reserved
sauce. Lightly cover with aluminum foil; bake at 400 degrees for
30 to 45 minutes. Sprinkle with Parmesan cheese.

Many comfort-food recipes make plenty of food for sharing.
Invite a neighbor or co-worker you've wanted to get to
know better...encourage your kids to invite a friend.
You'll be so glad you did!

Prize-Winning Pot Roast

Serves 4 to 6

3-1/2 to 5-lb. beef chuck roast
2 10-3/4 oz. cans cream of
  celery soup
1-1/2 oz. pkg. onion soup mix
1 to 2 c. red wine or beef broth
1/2 c. frozen apple juice
  concentrate
4 to 6 potatoes, peeled and
  quartered

4 to 8 carrots, peeled and cut
  into 3-inch pieces
1-lb. pkg. sliced mushrooms
8 stalks celery, chopped
1 t. salt
1/8 t. pepper

Place beef in a roasting pan; top with soup and soup mix. Stir in wine or broth; cover. Bake at 350 degrees for one hour; add apple juice, potatoes and carrots. Bake for another 30 minutes; remove from oven. Add mushrooms, celery, salt and pepper; bake for one additional hour, uncovering for the last 30 minutes.

There are so many satisfying ways to fix potatoes!
Whenever you boil potatoes, toss in a few extras...you'll have
a head start on your next potato dish.

Scalloped Potatoes & Ham

Serves 6 to 8

8 to 10 potatoes, peeled and
   sliced
2 c. cooked ham, cubed
1 onion, diced

1 c. shredded Cheddar cheese
pepper to taste
10-3/4 oz. can cream of
   mushroom soup

In a slow cooker, layer each ingredient in the order given, spreading
soup over top. Do not stir. Cover and cook on low setting for 8 to
10 hours, or on high setting for 5 hours.

Packages of prepared mashed potatoes from your grocer
are a quick & easy way to top Shepherd's Pie...
homemade taste without the work!

Shepherd's Pie

Makes 4 to 6 servings

2 lbs. ground beef
1/2 onion, chopped
.75-oz. pkg. brown gravy mix
2 10-3/4 oz. cans cream of
    mushroom soup
1 c. water

salt and pepper to taste
2-1/2 to 3 c. potatoes, peeled,
    boiled and mashed
8-oz. pkg. shredded Cheddar
    cheese

Brown ground beef and onion in a skillet over medium heat. Drain;
pour into a bowl. Stir in gravy mix, soup and water; mix well. Spread
in a greased 13"x9" baking pan or 9" deep-dish pie plate. Sprinkle
with salt and pepper. Spread potatoes over top; bake at 350 degrees
for 45 minutes. Sprinkle with cheese; bake for an additional
10 minutes, or until cheese is melted.

Vintage magazine recipe ads make fun wall art for
the kitchen. They're easy to find at flea markets...look for
ones featuring shimmery gelatin salads, golden mac & cheese
or other favorites like Mom used to make!

Easy Beef Goulash

Makes 4 to 6 servings

1/2 c. all-purpose flour
1 T. paprika
salt and pepper to taste
1 to 2 lbs. beef chuck steak,
    cut into 1-inch cubes

1 T. olive oil
6-oz. can tomato paste
1-1/2 oz. pkg. onion soup mix
cooked egg noodles

Combine flour, paprika, salt and pepper in a small bowl. Dredge beef cubes in mixture; brown beef in hot oil in a skillet. Place beef in a slow cooker; top with tomato paste and soup mix. Add just enough water to cover meat; stir to blend. Cover and cook on low setting for 5 to 6 hours. Serve over egg noodles.

Start family meals with a gratitude circle...each person takes a moment to share two or three things that he or she is thankful for that day. A sure way to put everyone in a cheerful mood!

Ham for a Houseful

Makes about 16 servings

20-oz. can crushed pineapple, drained
1 c. brown sugar, packed
2 T. honey

1/2 T. dry mustard
1/2 t. ground cloves
4 to 5-lb. fully cooked boneless ham

Combine all ingredients except ham in a large saucepan. Cook over medium heat until sugar dissolves, about 5 minutes. Stirring constantly, cook until liquid reduces and mixture thickens, about 10 more minutes; remove from heat to cool. Score surface of ham in a diamond pattern; insert meat thermometer into center of ham. Place ham in a roasting pan; cover and bake at 325 degrees for one hour. Uncover; spoon glaze over ham. Bake 45 minutes to one hour longer; or until meat thermometer reads 140 degrees; baste every 15 minutes with pan drippings.

Skillet gravy is super-easy to make. Melt a tablespoon of butter in a skillet over medium heat, then sprinkle in a tablespoon of all-purpose flour and whisk for one minute. Add a can of chicken or beef broth and a dash of pepper. Stir well, lower heat and simmer for about 5 minutes, until gravy is thickened.

Roast Chicken with Vegetables

Serves 6

3 to 3-1/2 lb. chicken
1 T. plus 1 t. olive oil, divided
1 t. dried thyme
1/2 t. salt
1/2 t. pepper
6 small white onions

6 carrots, peeled and cut into
  2-inch pieces
6 stalks celery, cut into 2-inch
  pieces
4 potatoes, peeled and cubed

Place chicken in a large shallow roasting pan. Tie the legs together with kitchen string; insert meat thermometer into thickest part of thigh without touching bone. Rub chicken with one teaspoon oil; sprinkle with thyme, salt and pepper. Bake, uncovered, at 475 degrees for 15 minutes. Toss vegetables with remaining oil; arrange around chicken. Reduce oven to 400 degrees; bake for an additional 35 to 45 minutes, until chicken's internal temperature reaches 170 degrees.

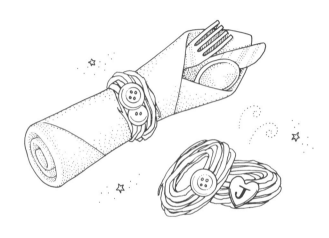

Quick & easy farmhouse napkin rings!
Glue a charm or button to a little grapevine ring
and slip in a cloth napkin.

Gramma's Smothered Swiss Steak

Serves 4 to 6

1 to 1-1/2 lbs. beef round
   steak, cut into serving-size
   pieces
1 to 2 T. oil
1 onion, halved and sliced
1 carrot, peeled and shredded

4-oz. can sliced mushrooms,
   drained
10-3/4 oz. can cream of
   mushroom soup
8-oz. can tomato sauce

Brown beef in oil in a skillet over medium heat; drain and set aside.
Arrange vegetables in a slow cooker; place beef on top. Mix together
soup and tomato sauce; pour over beef and vegetables. Cover and
cook on low setting for 8 hours, until beef is tender.

Alongside sticky, ooey-gooey comfort foods, set out a basket of warm, moistened washcloths. Dampen washcloths with water and a little lemon juice, roll up and microwave on high for 10 to 15 seconds. Guests will thank you!

Southern BBQ

Makes 6 to 8 sandwiches

1 c. cider vinegar
2 T. sugar
1 T. salt
3 to 4-lb. pork loin roast
1 T. Worcestershire sauce

1/2 c. catsup
Optional: hot pepper sauce to
   taste
6 to 8 sandwich buns, split

Mix together vinegar, sugar and salt. Pour over roast in a slow cooker. Cover and cook on low setting for 10 to 12 hours, until pork pulls from bones. Remove and cool; pull apart and shred. Mix 6 to 8 tablespoons of cooking liquid with Worcestershire sauce and catsup. Pour over pork and add hot sauce to taste, if desired; mix well. Spoon shredded pork and sauce onto buns.

Homemade coleslaw...scrumptious! Blend a bag of shredded coleslaw mix with 1/2 cup mayonnaise, 2 tablespoons milk, one tablespoon vinegar and 1/2 teaspoon sugar. For a yummy variation, toss in some pineapple tidbits or mandarin oranges. Chill before serving.

Mom's Sloppy Joes

Makes 8 to 10 servings

1 lb. ground beef
1/2 c. onion, chopped
1/2 c. celery, thinly sliced
1-1/2 c. catsup
1/4 c. brown sugar, packed

1 T. vinegar
1-1/2 T. mustard
salt and pepper to taste
8 to 10 sandwich buns, split

Brown beef with onion and celery in a skillet; drain and set aside.
Mix remaining ingredients except buns; add to beef mixture. Bring to
a boil; reduce heat and simmer until thoroughly warmed. Spoon onto
buns to serve.

Try something new...grilled cheese croutons! Make
grilled cheese sandwiches as usual, then slice them into small
squares. Toss into a bowl of creamy tomato soup...yum!

Old-Fashioned Tomato Soup

Serves 4 to 6

32-oz. can diced tomatoes
1 c. chicken broth
2 T. butter
2 T. sugar

1 T. onion, chopped
1/8 t. baking soda
2 c. light cream

Combine undrained tomatoes, broth, butter, sugar, onion and baking soda in a large saucepan. Simmer over low heat for one hour. Warm cream in a double boiler; add to hot tomato mixture. Blend well.

For thick, creamy vegetable or bean soup, use a hand-held immersion blender to purée some of the cooked veggies right in the soup pot.

Nana's Potato Soup

Makes 8 servings

1/2 c. butter
10 T. all-purpose flour
4 14-1/2 oz. cans chicken
    broth
1 T. fresh chives, chopped
1 T. fresh parsley, chopped
4 c. half-and-half

6 to 8 potatoes, peeled, cubed
    and cooked
salt and pepper to taste
Garnish: shredded Cheddar
    cheese, bacon bits, chopped
    green onions

Melt butter in a Dutch oven over medium heat. Stir in flour, one tablespoon at a time, until smooth. Add broth, chives and parsley; stir until thickened. Add half-and-half, stirring until well mixed. Stir in potatoes and heat through; sprinkle to taste with salt and pepper. Garnish as desired.

Adapt a family favorite soup, stew or chili to the slow cooker.
A recipe that simmers for 2 hours on the stovetop can generally
cook all day on the low setting without overcooking.

Vegetable Soup

Serves 6 to 8

8 c. water
2 t. salt
1/4 t. pepper
1 t. sugar
6 carrots, peeled and diced
3 stalks celery, diced
4 onions, diced

1/4 cabbage, shredded
1 c. tomatoes, diced
4 sprigs fresh parsley
2 cubes vegetable or beef
   bouillon
Garnish: saltine crackers

In a stockpot over medium-high heat, combine water, salt, pepper and sugar. Bring to a boil. Add vegetables and parsley. Reduce heat to medium and simmer one hour. Add bouillon cubes; remove from heat and stir until bouillon is completely dissolved. Serve very hot with crackers.

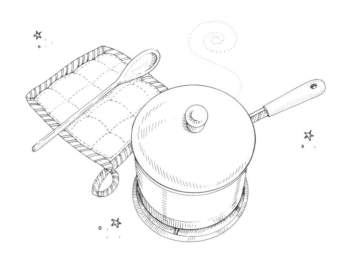

Add big, fluffy dumplings to your favorite stew. When the stew is nearly finished cooking, top with refrigerated biscuits and continue simmering for 10 to 15 minutes, until done.

Lillian's Beef Stew

Serves 8

2 lbs. stew beef, cubed
2 potatoes, peeled and
   quartered
3 stalks celery, diced
4 carrots, peeled and thickly
   sliced
2 onions, quartered

2 c. cocktail vegetable juice
1/3 c. quick-cooking tapioca,
   uncooked
1 T. sugar
1 T. salt
1/2 t. dried basil
1/4 t. pepper

Arrange beef and vegetables in slow cooker. Combine remaining
ingredients; pour into slow cooker. Cover and cook on low setting for
8 to 10 hours.

Make a savory meal even better! Serve up a favorite soup
or stew in hollowed-out round loaves of crusty bread...
so cozy shared in front of a crackling fire.

Comfort Chicken Soup

Serves 6

8 c. water
8 cubes chicken bouillon
6-1/2 c. wide egg noodles,
    uncooked
2 10-3/4 oz. cans cream of
    chicken soup

3 c. cooked chicken, cubed
8-oz. container sour cream
Garnish: dried parsley to taste

Bring water and bouillon to a boil in a large soup pot over medium-high heat. Add noodles and simmer, uncovered, for 10 minutes. Stir in soup and chicken; heat through. Remove soup pot from heat; add sour cream. Sprinkle with parsley to taste.

The most indispensable ingredient of all good home cooking:
love, for those you are cooking for.

-Sophia Loren

Rich & Meaty Chili

Serves 6 to 8

1 lb. ground beef
1/2 c. onion, chopped
2 T. butter
2 15-1/2 oz. cans kidney beans
2 15-oz. cans chili beans
4 c. tomatoes, diced
6-oz. can tomato paste
2 to 3 t. chili powder
1-1/2 t. salt
1/2 t. dried oregano
1/4 t. pepper
1/8 t. hot pepper sauce
1 bay leaf
1-1/2 c. water
1 c. celery, chopped
1 c. green pepper, chopped
Garnish: shredded Cheddar
          cheese, sour cream

In a Dutch oven over medium-high heat, brown ground beef with
onion in butter; drain. Stir in remaining ingredients except garnish.
Bring to a boil; reduce heat and simmer for one hour. Remove bay
leaf before serving. Spoon into serving bowls; garnish with cheese
and sour cream.

Crunchy toppings can really add fun and flavor to soup
or chili. Some fun choices...fish-shaped crackers, bacon bits,
French fried onions, sunflower seeds or toasted nuts.

Old-Fashioned Ham & Bean Soup

Serves 4 to 6

2 meaty ham hocks or 1 meaty
    ham bone
16-oz. pkg. dried navy beans
1 c. cooked ham, chopped
1/2 to 3/4 c. onion, quartered
    and sliced
3 stalks celery, chopped

1/2 c. carrot, peeled and grated
2 bay leaves
1/2 t. garlic powder
1/2 t. seasoned salt
1/4 t. pepper
1/2 t. dried parsley
1/8 t. dried thyme

The night before, cover ham hocks or ham bone with water in a large stockpot. Simmer over medium heat until tender. Remove ham hocks or bone from stockpot, reserving broth; slice off ham. Refrigerate reserved broth and meat overnight. Cover beans with water in a bowl and let stand overnight. The next day, drain beans and set aside. Discard fat from top of reserved broth; add beans, ham, and remaining ingredients to broth. Bring to a boil. Reduce heat; simmer until beans are tender and soup is desired thickness, about one hour. Discard bay leaves.

Whip up a loaf of beer bread for dinner. Combine 2 cups
self-rising flour, a 12-ounce can of beer and 3 tablespoons sugar
in a greased loaf pan. Bake for 25 minutes at 350 degrees,
then drizzle with melted butter. Warm and tasty!

Prairie Bacon-Corn Chowder

Serves 10 to 12

1 lb. bacon, chopped
4 c. potatoes, peeled and diced
2 c. onion, chopped
1/2 c. water
2 10-3/4 oz. cans cream of
    chicken soup

2 15-1/4 oz. cans corn, drained
16-oz. container sour cream
2-1/2 c. milk

In a skillet over medium-high heat, cook bacon for 5 minutes; drain.
Add potatoes, onion and water to skillet. Cook for 15 to 20 minutes
until tender, stirring occasionally. Drain; transfer mixture to a slow
cooker. Combine remaining ingredients; add to slow cooker and stir
to blend. Cover and cook on low setting for 2 hours.

Making butter is fun for kids. Pour a pint of heavy cream into a chilled wide-mouth jar, cap the jar tightly and take turns shaking until you see butter begin to form. When it's done, uncap the jar and rinse the butter lightly with cool water. Enjoy on warm, fresh-baked bread...scrumptious!

Best-Ever Banana Bread

Makes 6 mini loaves

1/2 c. shortening
1 c. sugar
2 eggs
3/4 c. ripe banana, mashed

1-1/4 c. cake flour
3/4 t. baking soda
1/2 t. salt

In a large bowl, blend shortening and sugar well. Add eggs, one at a time, beating well after each; stir in banana and set aside. Stir together flour, baking soda and salt in a separate bowl; add to shortening mixture and mix well. Pour into 6 greased 5-1/2"x3" mini loaf pans. Bake at 350 degrees for 40 to 45 minutes.

The aroma of bread baking is so comforting...even refrigerated rolls will make your kitchen smell heavenly. Dress up rolls with a drizzle of melted butter and a dash of dried oregano before baking...almost as good as homemade!

Farmhouse Bread

Makes 4 loaves

2 T. active dry yeast
1 c. warm water, 110 to
    115 degrees
4 c. warm milk
1/2 c. oil

6 T. sugar
2 T. salt
2-1/2 c. whole-wheat flour
8-1/2 c. all-purpose flour,
    divided

Sprinkle yeast into warm water; set aside. In a large bowl, combine milk, oil, sugar and salt; add wheat flour and 2-1/2 cups all-purpose flour. Mix in yeast mixture; add remaining flour. Let rest for 10 minutes; knead for 5 minutes. Allow dough to double in bulk; punch down and allow to double in bulk again. Divide dough into quarters; place into 4 greased 9"x5" loaf pans and let double once more. Bake at 400 degrees for 5 minutes; reduce heat to 375 degrees and bake for 5 minutes; reduce heat to 350 degrees and bake for 20 minutes; reduce heat to 325 degrees and bake for 5 minutes.

Keep bread or rolls nice and warm during dinner. Before arranging
rolls in a bread basket, place a terra-cotta warming tile
in the bottom and line with a homespun tea towel.
Now pass the butter, please!

Nana's Biscuits

Makes 2-1/2 dozen

4 c. all-purpose flour
2 T. baking powder
2 t. salt

1/2 c. shortening
2 c. milk
2 T. butter, melted

Combine flour, baking powder and salt; cut in shortening with 2 forks or a pastry cutter. Stir in milk; roll out to 1/2-inch thickness on a lightly floured surface. Cut with a biscuit cutter; arrange in an ungreased 13"x9" baking pan. Drizzle with butter; bake at 450 degrees for 15 to 20 minutes, until golden.

Give homebaked breads a mouthwatering golden finish.
Whisk together an egg yolk and a tablespoon of water in a cup.
Brush the mixture over the dough just before popping it
into the oven...that's it!

Butterfly Yeast Rolls

Makes one dozen

1 env. active dry yeast
1/4 c. warm water, 110 to
   115 degrees
1 c. milk
1/4 c. sugar

1/4 c. shortening
1 t. salt
3-1/2 c. all-purpose flour,
   divided
1 egg, beaten

In a small bowl, mix yeast with warm water; let stand for 5 minutes. Heat milk in a small saucepan over low heat just until boiling; let cool slightly. In a large bowl, combine milk, sugar, shortening and salt. Add 1-1/2 cups flour and beat well. Beat in yeast mixture and egg. Gradually knead in remaining flour to form a soft dough. Place in a greased bowl, turning once. Cover and let rise in a warm place for 2 hours. Punch dough down; turn out on a floured surface. Shape into 36 walnut-size balls; place 3 balls in each of 12 greased muffin cups. Cover and let rise for 45 minutes. Bake at 400 degrees for 12 to 15 minutes, or until golden.

Whip up a crock of Honey Butter to serve with warm cornbread or rolls. Simply combine one cup honey with one cup softened butter and one teaspoon vanilla extract.

Honey-Corn Muffins

Makes 9 to 12

1 c. yellow cornmeal
1/4 c. all-purpose flour
1-1/2 t. baking powder
1 egg, beaten
1/3 c. milk

1/4 c. corn
1/4 c. honey
3 T. butter, melted
Garnish: Honey Butter
(opposite page)

Mix together cornmeal, flour and baking powder; set aside. In a separate bowl, combine egg, milk, corn, honey and butter. Add egg mixture to cornmeal mixture, stirring just enough to moisten. Fill paper-lined muffin cups 2/3 full. Bake at 400 degrees for about 20 minutes. Serve with Honey Butter.

There are so many ways to serve mashed potatoes! Spoon them over a casserole for a quick shepherd's pie, turn them into crispy potato pancakes or scoop into a bowl and top with gravy, chopped chicken and corn for a homestyle dinner-in-a-bowl.

Grandma's Buttery Mashed Potatoes *Serves 8 to 12*

6 to 8 potatoes, peeled and
    cubed
1/2 c. butter, softened

1 c. evaporated milk
salt and pepper to taste

Cover potatoes with water in a large saucepan; bring to a boil over
medium-high heat. Cook until tender, about 15 minutes; drain. Add
remaining ingredients. Beat with an electric mixer on medium speed
until blended and creamy.

Casseroles spell comfort food...but what if the recipe is large
and your family is small? Simple... just divide the ingredients into
two small dishes and freeze one for later!

Potluck Potato Bake

Makes 8 to 10 servings

32-oz. pkg. frozen diced
    potatoes, thawed
16-oz. container sour cream
1 onion, chopped
8-oz. pkg. shredded Cheddar
    cheese

10-3/4 oz. can cream of celery
    soup
3/4 c. butter, melted and
    divided
2 c. corn flake cereal, crushed

In a large bowl, stir together potatoes, sour cream, onion, cheese, soup and 1/4 cup butter. Pour into a greased 13"x9" baking pan. In a separate bowl, toss cereal and remaining butter together; spread over top of casserole. Bake, covered, at 350 degrees for one hour and 15 minutes. Uncover and bake for an additional 15 minutes.

When frying bacon for this recipe, reserve a few pieces.
Slice a homegrown tomato into thick slices and add crisp lettuce
and country-style bread for a fresh BLT sandwich...
tomorrow's lunch is ready!

Country Baked Beans

Serves 10 to 12

1 lb. bacon, diced
1 onion, chopped
56-oz. can pork & beans
1/4 c. molasses
1 T. vinegar

1/2 t. salt
1/4 c. brown sugar, packed
1/4 c. catsup
1/2 T. mustard

In a skillet over medium heat, cook bacon with onion until crisp;
drain and crumble. Combine with remaining ingredients in an
ungreased 3-1/2 quart casserole dish. Bake, uncovered, at
300 degrees for 1-1/2 hours.

Search out fun retro tablecloths
at flea markets and tag sales...
they're often found for a song. Buy a bunch...they'll bring
a burst of color and whimsy to table settings!

Dad's Best Mac & Cheese

Makes 6 to 8 servings

8-oz. pkg. elbow macaroni,
  uncooked
1 egg, beaten
1 T. hot water
1 t. dry mustard

1 t. salt
1 c. milk
12-oz. pkg. shredded sharp
  Cheddar cheese, divided
1 T. butter, softened

Cook macaroni according to package directions; drain and return to pan. Whisk egg, water, mustard and salt together; add to macaroni. Pour in milk and stir well. Add most of cheese, reserving enough to sprinkle on top. Spread butter in a 2-quart casserole dish; pour macaroni mixture into dish. Sprinkle with reserved cheese. Bake, uncovered, at 350 degrees for 35 to 45 minutes, until top is golden.

Look for heirloom fruits & vegetables at farmers' markets...
varieties that Grandma & Grandpa may have grown in their
garden. These fruits and veggies don't always look
picture-perfect but their flavor can't be beat!

Libby's Southern Green Beans

Serves 6 to 8

1/2 c. bacon drippings
2 to 2-1/2 lbs. green beans, cut
   lengthwise

salt and pepper to taste

Melt drippings in a large cast-iron skillet; add beans. Simmer on low heat, covered, for 3 to 4 hours, stirring 3 to 4 times to cook evenly. During the last 30 minutes, uncover and brown lightly. Add salt and pepper to taste.

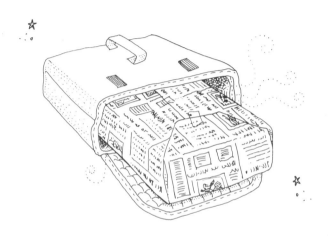

Taking a favorite dish along to a potluck or picnic?
Keep it toasty warm...cover the casserole dish with aluminum foil,
then wrap it in several layers of newspaper.

Country Corn Pudding

Makes 8 servings

16-oz. pkg. frozen corn
2 11-oz. cans sweet corn &
   diced peppers
14-3/4 oz. can creamed corn

6-1/2 oz. pkg. corn muffin mix
3/4 c. water
1/4 c. butter, melted
1 t. salt

Mix all ingredients well; pour into a slow cooker. Cover and cook on low setting for 5 to 6 hours, stirring after 3 hours.

To cover or not to cover? A casserole that's baked uncovered will have a crisper, more golden topping than one that's covered during baking...it's your choice.

Broccoli-Cheese Casserole

Serves 8 to 10

1 c. celery, chopped
1 onion, chopped
1/4 c. butter
1-1/2 c. cooked rice
10-oz. pkg. frozen chopped
　broccoli, thawed

8-oz. can sliced water
　chestnuts, drained
10-3/4 oz. can cream of
　mushroom soup
8-oz. jar pasteurized process
　cheese sauce

In a saucepan over medium heat, sauté celery and onion in butter.
Stir in remaining ingredients; spread in a greased 13"x9" baking pan.
Bake, uncovered, at 350 degrees for 45 minutes.

Make a cozy, quick & easy fleece throw for your sofa.
Buy a 2-yard length of colorful fleece and cut 6-inch fringes
along each edge...why not make an extra for a friend?

Pineapple Casserole

Serves 4

1/2 c. sugar
3 T. all-purpose flour
1 c. shredded Cheddar cheese
20-oz. can pineapple chunks,
    drained and 3 T. juice
    reserved

1/2 c. round buttery crackers,
    crushed
1/4 c. butter, melted

Stir together sugar and flour in a large bowl; gradually stir in cheese. Add pineapple; mix well. Spoon into a greased 1-1/2 quart casserole dish. In a separate bowl, combine cracker crumbs, melted butter and reserved pineapple juice until well blended. Sprinkle cracker mixture over pineapple mixture. Bake, uncovered, at 350 degrees for 20 to 30 minutes, until golden.

Need a snack to tide the kids over until dinner?
Head to the pantry and mix up mini pretzels, crunchy cereal
squares, raisins and nuts...toss in a few candy-coated
chocolates for fun and let them enjoy!

Suzie-Q Candied Carrots

Serves 8 to 10

2 lbs. carrots, peeled and sliced 1/2 t. vanilla extract
1/2 c. butter 1/2 t. pepper
1 c. brown sugar, packed

Place carrots in a large saucepan; cover with water. Bring to a boil over medium-high heat. Cook until fork-tender; drain. Add butter, brown sugar, vanilla and pepper; simmer over medium heat until thickened, about 5 minutes.

Keep a couple of favorite side dishes tucked away in the freezer.
Pair with hot sandwiches or a deli roast chicken to put a hearty
homestyle meal on the table in a hurry.

Nutty Sweet Potato Casserole

Serves 10 to 12

3 c. sweet potatoes, peeled,
    boiled and mashed
1/2 c. sugar
1 c. butter, melted and divided
1/2 c. milk

2 eggs, beaten
1 t. vanilla extract
1 c. brown sugar, packed
1/2 c. all-purpose flour
1 c. chopped pecans

Combine sweet potatoes, sugar, 1/2 cup butter, milk, eggs and vanilla. Mix well; spoon into a greased 13"x9" baking pan and set aside. Mix remaining butter and other ingredients together; sprinkle over potato mixture. Bake, uncovered, at 350 degrees for 25 minutes.

For a simple, sweetly scented place setting, tie a few cinnamon sticks together with raffia, attach a mailing label as a name card and lay a bundle across each plate.

Brown Sugar Applesauce

Makes 6 to 8 servings

3 lbs. cooking apples, cored,
    peeled and sliced
1/2 c. brown sugar, packed

1 t. cinnamon
1-1/2 T. lemon juice
Garnish: cinnamon

Combine all ingredients except garnish in a slow cooker. Cover and cook on high setting for 3 hours. Stir occasionally; mash with a potato masher to desired consistency. Sprinkle portions with cinnamon.

Yogurt is a great healthy substitute for sour cream. Try vanilla or fruit-flavored yogurt in sweet dishes like ambrosia and plain yogurt in savory main dishes.

Ambrosia

Makes 6 to 8 servings

1 T. sugar
1 c. sour cream
1 c. mini marshmallows

1 c. crushed pineapple, drained
1 c. sweetened flaked coconut
1 c. mandarin oranges, drained

In a large serving bowl, stir sugar into sour cream; add remaining ingredients. Stir well; chill.

If you're short on table space when entertaining, an old-fashioned wooden ironing board makes a sturdy sideboard. Just adjust it to a convenient height, add a pretty table runner and set out the food...come & get it!

Mimi's Potato Salad

Makes 8 to 10 servings

3 lbs. potatoes, halved
1/2 c. Italian salad dressing
1 stalk celery, chopped
1 green onion, chopped
1/2 c. mayonnaise
salt and pepper to taste

2 radishes, thinly sliced
1 egg, hard-boiled, peeled and
  sliced
Garnish: paprika, fresh parsley
  sprigs

In a large saucepan, cover potatoes with water. Bring to a boil over high heat and boil until fork-tender, 15 to 20 minutes. Drain potatoes; while still warm, peel carefully. Cut potatoes into cubes and place in a large salad bowl. Drizzle salad dressing over warm potatoes; stir gently to coat. Let potatoes stand to absorb dressing. Add celery, green onion, mayonnaise, salt and pepper; toss gently. Arrange radish slices over potato salad; top with egg slices. Sprinkle with paprika; add parsley around edges. Serve chilled.

A small house will hold as much happiness as a big one.

-Anonymous

7-Layer Overnight Salad

Makes 8 to 10 servings

1 head lettuce, torn into
    bite-size pieces
1 to 2 onions, thinly sliced and
    separated into rings
10-oz. pkg. frozen peas
3 to 4 eggs, hard-boiled, peeled
    and sliced

4-oz. jar bacon bits
8-oz. jar mayonnaise
1-1/2 c. grated Parmesan
    cheese

Arrange 1/3 of lettuce in a large bowl. Top with 1/3 each of the
onions, frozen peas, eggs and bacon bits. Repeat layering twice.
Spoon mayonnaise completely over top; sprinkle with Parmesan.
Cover and refrigerate overnight.

Taking a salad to a picnic or potluck? Mix it up in a plastic zipping bag instead of a bowl, seal and set it right in the cooler. No worries about spills or leaks!

Mother's Cucumber Salad

Serves 6

3 to 4 cucumbers, peeled and
  thinly sliced
3 T. salt
2 t. sugar
1/2 t. onion powder

1/4 t. celery seed
1/4 t. pepper
1/4 c. cider vinegar
Optional: 1/2 c. sliced red onion

Place cucumbers in a large bowl; add salt and enough water to cover.
Cover and shake to mix salt. Refrigerate several hours to overnight.
Drain cucumbers, but do not rinse; return to bowl. Stir together sugar,
onion powder, celery seed, pepper and vinegar; mix well. Pour
vinegar mixture over top of cucumbers. Add onion, if desired. Cover
and shake gently to mix.

Set out some fun toppers for your after-dinner coffee...vanilla powder, whipped topping, mini chocolate chips and mini marshmallows. Yum!

Marsha's Cheery Cherry Salad

Serves 6 to 8

15-oz. can tart cherries, drained and juice reserved
8-1/2 oz. can crushed pineapple, drained and juice reserved
1/2 c. sugar

2 3-oz. pkgs. cherry gelatin mix
1-1/2 c. ginger ale
Optional: 1/2 c. chopped pecans
Garnish: whipped topping

Pour reserved cherry and pineapple juices into a 2-cup measuring cup. Add enough water to equal 1-3/4 cups. Pour into a small saucepan and add sugar. Bring to a boil over medium heat; stir in gelatin mix. Remove from heat; add fruit and ginger ale. Pour into a large serving bowl; chill in refrigerator until thickened, but not completely set. Stir in pecans, if desired. Return to refrigerator until fully set. Serve with whipped topping.

Fresh from the Kitchen of

Baked for YOU with L♥VE!

Copy, color, share!

Shirley's Chocolate Chip Cookies

Makes 4 dozen

1/2 c. shortening
6 T. sugar
6 T. brown sugar, packed
1 egg, beaten
1/2 t. vanilla extract

1-1/8 c. all-purpose flour
1/2 t. baking soda
1/2 t. salt
1 c. semi-sweet chocolate chips

Blend together shortening and sugars; stir in egg and vanilla. Add flour, baking soda and salt; mix well. Stir in chocolate chips. Drop by teaspoonfuls onto ungreased baking sheets. Bake at 375 degrees for 10 to 12 minutes, until lightly golden.

Share the delight of baking with children for memories in the making! Cut-out cookies are a great choice for budding bakers, with lots of fun shapes to choose from and brightly colored sweet trimmings galore.

Frosted Sugar Cookies

Makes 4 dozen

2 c. butter, softened
1-1/3 c. sugar
2 eggs, beaten

2 t. vanilla extract
5 c. all-purpose flour
Garnish: colored sugar

Blend butter and sugar together; stir in eggs and vanilla. Add flour; mix until well blended. Form into a ball; cover and chill for 4 hours to overnight. Roll out dough 1/4-inch thick on a lightly floured surface; cut out with cookie cutters as desired. Arrange cookies on lightly greased baking sheets. Bake at 350 degrees for 8 to 10 minutes, until golden. Frost cookies when cool; decorate as desired.

Frosting:

4-1/2 c. powdered sugar
6 T. butter, melted
6 T. milk

2 T. vanilla extract
1 T. lemon juice
Optional: food coloring

Combine all ingredients in a medium bowl. Beat with an electric mixer on low speed until smooth.

Fill a pretty tin with fresh-baked cookies. A welcome gift for new moms, college students and newlyweds...in fact, just about anyone! Don't forget to include the recipe too.

Classic Raisin Oatmeal Cookies

Makes 3 dozen

3/4 c. butter, softened
1 c. brown sugar, packed
1/2 c. sugar
1/4 c. milk
1 egg, beaten
1 t. vanilla extract
1 c. all-purpose flour

1 t. cinnamon
1/2 t. baking soda
1/4 t. salt
3 c. long-cooking oats, uncooked
1 c. chopped walnuts
1 c. raisins

Combine butter, sugars, milk, egg and vanilla in a large bowl. Beat until light and fluffy; set aside. Whisk together flour, cinnamon, baking soda and salt. Add to butter mixture; stir well. Add oats, walnuts and raisins. Drop by teaspoonfuls onto greased baking sheets. Bake in upper third of oven at 350 degrees for 12 to 15 minutes.

Serve brownie sundaes for an extra-special treat. Place brownies on individual dessert plates and top with a scoop of ice cream, a dollop of whipped topping and a cherry. Yummy!

Double-Chocolate Brownies

Makes one dozen

3 1-oz. sqs. unsweetened
   baking chocolate
6 T. butter
2/3 c. all-purpose flour
1/8 t. salt

1-1/3 c. sugar
3 eggs, beaten
1 t. vanilla extract
3/4 c. semi-sweet chocolate
   chips

Melt together unsweetened chocolate and butter in a small, heavy saucepan over low heat. Stir until smooth; remove from heat and let cool slightly. Stir together flour and salt; set aside. Gradually stir sugar into cooled chocolate mixture. Add eggs and vanilla; stir just to combine. Fold in flour mixture. Spread in an 8"x8" baking pan sprayed with non-stick vegetable spray. Sprinkle with chocolate chips; bake at 325 degrees for 30 to 35 minutes. Use a knife to spread melted chips over the surface. Let cool; cut into squares.

Offer mini portions of rich cake, cobbler or pie. Guests can take "just a taste" of something sweet after a big dinner or sample several yummy treats.

Triple Chocolate Delight

Makes 8 to 10 servings

18-1/2 oz. pkg. chocolate cake
    mix
3.9-oz. pkg. instant chocolate
    pudding mix
2 c. sour cream
1 c. water

1/2 c. oil
4 eggs, beaten
6-oz. pkg. semi-sweet chocolate
    chips
Garnish: vanilla ice cream or
    whipped topping

Combine all ingredients except garnish. Mix well and pour into a
greased slow cooker. Cover and cook for 6 to 8 hours at low setting.
Serve warm, garnished as desired.

Try new sugar-substitute blends made especially for baking up sweet, golden, moist goodies with half the sugar...there's even a brown sugar variety! Be sure to check the package for how to measure correctly.

Butterscotch Pie

Serves 8

2 c. milk
3 egg yolks
1/4 c. butter
1 T. all-purpose flour

1 c. brown sugar, packed
9-inch pie crust, baked
Optional: whipped topping

Whisk milk and egg yolks together; pour into a saucepan. Cook over low heat until warmed; remove from heat. Brown butter in a deep skillet over medium-low heat; stir in flour until smooth. Blend in sugar until dissolved; slowly add milk mixture, stirring until thickened, about 5 minutes. Pour into pie crust; refrigerate until firm. Serve with whipped topping, if desired.

A Grandma-style treat...roll out extra pie crust, cut into strips and sprinkle with cinnamon-sugar. Bake at 350 degrees until golden.

Easy Apple Crisp

Serves 8

4 c. cooking apples, cored,
    peeled and sliced
1/2 c. brown sugar, packed
1/2 c. quick-cooking oats,
    uncooked

1/3 c. all-purpose flour
3/4 t. cinnamon
1/4 c. butter, softened
Garnish: whipped topping,
    cinnamon

Arrange apple slices in a greased 11"x8" baking pan; set aside.
Combine remaining ingredients; stir until crumbly and sprinkle over
apples. Bake at 350 degrees for 30 to 35 minutes. Serve portions
topped with a dollop of whipped topping and a sprinkle of cinnamon.

Watch for vintage plates at tag sales. They're just the thing for delivering cookies to friends & neighbors...the recipient will feel extra-special and the dish is hers to keep.

Sundown Cobbler

Makes 6 to 8 servings

1/2 c. butter
1 c. self-rising flour
1 c. sugar

1 c. milk
2 to 2-1/2 c. peaches, pitted
  and sliced

Melt butter in a greased 2-quart casserole dish. In a large bowl, combine flour, sugar and milk; pour over butter, but do not mix. Add peaches; do not mix. Bake, uncovered, at 350 degrees for one hour. Serve warm.

Make dessert extra special with a dollop of sweetened whipped cream. Beat together 1/2 pint whipping cream with one tablespoon sugar and one teaspoon vanilla until soft peaks form. Scrumptious!

Creamy Banana Pudding

Makes 8 to 10 servings

5-1/4 oz. pkg. instant vanilla
    pudding mix
2 c. milk
14-oz. can sweetened
    condensed milk

12-oz. container frozen
    whipped topping, thawed
12-oz. pkg. vanilla wafers
4 to 5 bananas, sliced

Combine pudding mix, milks and topping in a large bowl; mix
together until well blended. Spoon one cup of pudding mixture into a
large glass serving bowl. Layer with 1/3 each of wafers, banana
slices and remaining pudding mixture. Repeat layers twice, ending
with pudding mixture. Chill; keep refrigerated.

INDEX

INDEX

Our Story

Back in 1984, we were next-door neighbors raising our families in the little town of Delaware, Ohio. Two moms with small children, we were looking for a way to do what we loved and stay home with the kids too. We had always shared a love of home cooking and making memories with family & friends and so, after many a conversation over the backyard fence, **Gooseberry Patch** was born.

We put together our first catalog at our kitchen tables, enlisting the help of our loved ones wherever we could. From that very first mailing, we found an immediate connection with many of our customers and it wasn't long before we began receiving letters, photos and recipes from these new friends. In 1992, we put together our very first cookbook, compiled from hundreds of these recipes and, the rest, as they say, is history.

Hard to believe it's been over 30 years since those kitchen-table days! From that original little **Gooseberry Patch** family, we've grown to include an amazing group of creative folks who love cooking, decorating and creating as much as we do. Today, we're best known for our homestyle, family-friendly cookbooks, now recognized as national bestsellers.

One thing's for sure, we couldn't have done it without our friends all across the country. Each year, we're honored to turn thousands of your recipes into our collectible cookbooks. Our hope is that each book captures the stories and heart of all of you who have shared with us. Whether you've been with us since the beginning or are just discovering us, welcome to the **Gooseberry Patch** family!

Visit our website anytime
www.gooseberrypatch.com

Email

1·800·854·6673

Vickie & JoAnn